Cool and Refreshing

SUMMER DRINKS

Les Ilagan

DISCLAIMER

Content Arcade Publishing and its authors are joined together to create these pages and their publications. Content Arcade Publishing and its authors make no assurance of any kind, stated or implied, concerning the information provided.

LIMITS OF LIABILITY

Content Arcade Publishing and its authors shall not be held legally responsible in the event of incidental or consequential damages in line with or arising out of supplying the information presented here.

TABLE OF CONTENTS

INTRODUCTION

This book provides a collection of iced drink and smoothie recipes that are great for keeping you cool during the hot summer months. Included here are refreshing beverages made with fruits that are abundant during the summer season, like citrus fruits, berries, and melons. These drinks are delicious any time of day, especially when the weather gets hot because they can help cool you down and rehydrate your body.

Summer fruits are naturally sweet, making them ideal for creating mocktails, juices, coolers, or smoothies. This book will give you plenty of options using different fruits and other ingredients to make sure you get that cool and refreshing feeling.

Iced beverages or coolers complement any meal, whether for breakfast, lunch, or dinner. While smoothies can be enjoyed as a quick meal for breakfast or snack because they are nutritious and filling.

To make homemade fruit-based summer drinks, start with real fruit. Fresh fruits taste better and are healthier than most store-bought juices. So for the best flavor and nutrition, choose the freshest fruit available instead of using a concentrate. And, of course, feel free to adjust the sweetener to your liking.

Make a batch of these summer drinks and keep them

on hand while you're traveling this summer. Tip: Freeze some fruits in ice trays for a fun garnish.

The recipes in this book are fun to prepare and can be enjoyed by kids too. So, let your kids join you in the kitchen to give them a sense of responsibility while they create their own summer coolers and smoothies.

How to Prepare a Simple Sugar Syrup for Beverages

If you have a sweet tooth, you will probably need to add a sweetener to your iced drinks, smoothies, and other beverages. Here is a basic recipe for making a simple sugar syrup:

You will need:
1 cup (200 g) granulated white sugar
1 cup (250 ml) water
A small pot or saucepan

Method:
1.   In a small pot or saucepan, combine the sugar and water. Bring to a boil over medium-high heat for 4 to 5 minutes or until the sugar is dissolved completely. Let it cool to room temperature.
2.   Transfer to a sealed container or bottle if not using right away. Keep refrigerated.

While some of us love to indulge in a fruity summer cocktail, sometimes you need a drink that's completely alcohol-free. So it's time to try these mocktails and iced beverage recipes if you want something refreshing and delicious this summer.

These fun and fruity recipes will give you all the summer vibes without the hangover!

ALCOHOL-FREE STRAWBERRY MOJITO

Preparation Time	Total Time	Yield
5 minutes	5 minutes	4 servings

INGREDIENTS

- 2 ½ cups (500 g) fresh strawberries, hulled and sliced
- 1 medium (85 g) lemon
- 1 handful spearmint leaves
- 2 cups (480 ml) sparkling water
- 1/3 cup (80 ml) simple sugar syrup
- Ice cubes, to serve
- Mint sprigs, for garnish

METHOD

- Cut the lemon into thin rounds. Place them in a sturdy pitcher.
- Add the mint leaves and half of the strawberries. Crush to release the oils from the lemon and mint using a muddler.
- Stir in water, remaining strawberries and sugar syrup. Mix until everything is blended well.
- Pour in serving glasses over ice cubes. Do not strain. Garnish with mint sprigs.
- Serve immediately and enjoy.

NUTRITIONAL INFORMATION

Energy	Fat	Carbohydrates	Protein	Sodium
82 calories	0.3 g	21.4 g	0.8 g	3 mg

ALCOHOL-FREE LIMEADE MOJITO

Preparation Time	Total Time	Yield
5 minutes	5 minutes	4 servings

INGREDIENTS

- 1 medium (70 g) lime, juiced
- 32 fl. oz. (960 ml) sparkling water
- 1/3 cup (80 ml) simple sugar syrup
- 1 handful of fresh mint leaves
- Lime slices, to serve
- Ice cubes, to serve

METHOD

- Combine the lime juice, sparkling water, and sugar syrup in a pitcher. Mix well.
- Add the lime slices, mint leaves, and ice cubes. Stir.
- Pour in serving glasses.
- Serve immediately and enjoy.

NUTRITIONAL INFORMATION

Energy	Fat	Carbohydrates	Protein	Sodium
52 calories	0.0 g	14.3 g	0.1 g	0 mg

ALCOHOL-FREE WATERMELON MOJITO

Preparation Time	Total Time	Yield
5 minutes	5 minutes	4 servings

INGREDIENTS

- 3 cups (450 g) watermelon, cubed
- 1 medium (85 g) lemon
- 1 handful spearmint leaves
- 2 cups (480 ml) sparkling water
- 1/3 cup (80 ml) simple sugar syrup
- Ice cubes, to serve
- Mint sprigs, for garnish

METHOD

- Cut the lemon into thin rounds. Place them in a sturdy pitcher.
- Add the mint leaves and watermelon. Crush to release the flavor from the watermelon and the oils from the lemon and mint using a muddler.
- Stir in sparkling water and sugar syrup. Mix until everything is blended well.
- Pour in serving glasses over ice cubes. Do not strain. Garnish with mint sprigs.
- Serve immediately and enjoy.

NUTRITIONAL INFORMATION

Energy	Fat	Carbohydrates	Protein	Sodium
87 calories	0.2 g	23.0 g	0.9 g	3 mg

ALCOHOL-FREE MARGARITA

Preparation Time	Total Time	Yield
5 minutes	5 minutes	4 servings

INGREDIENTS

- 1/2 cup (120 ml) orange juice
- 1/3 cup (80 ml) lime juice
- 2 cups (480 ml) lemon-flavored sparkling water
- 1 cup (240 ml) lime-flavored sparkling water
- 1/3 cup (80 ml) simple sugar syrup
- Crushed ice, to serve
- Salt, to serve
- Mint sprigs, for garnish

METHOD

- Combine the lime juice, orange juice, sparkling water, and sugar syrup in a pitcher.
- Rim each glass with salt by turning the glass upside down and dipping it into water and then salt.
- Fill 2/3 of the glasses with crushed ice. Then, pour the margarita mixture. Garnish with mint sprigs.
- Serve immediately and enjoy.

NUTRITIONAL INFORMATION

Energy	Fat	Carbohydrates	Protein	Sodium
79 calories	0.1 g	20.8 g	0.3 g	2 mg

BERRY AND CITRUS MOCKTAIL

Preparation Time	Total Time	Yield
5 minutes	5 minutes	4 servings

INGREDIENTS

- 1 cup (200 g) fresh strawberries, hulled and quartered
- 1 cup (100 g) fresh cranberries
- 1 cup (240 ml) orange juice
- 1 cup (240 ml) cranberry juice
- 1 cup (240 ml) cold water
- 1/4 cup (60 ml) lime juice
- 1/4 cup (60 ml) grenadine syrup
- Ice cubes, to serve
- Orange wedges, for garnish

METHOD

- Place the strawberries, cranberries, orange juice, cranberry juice, water, lime juice, and grenadine syrup in a pitcher. Mix until blended well.
- Pour in serving glasses with ice cubes. Garnish with orange wedges.
- Serve immediately and enjoy.

NUTRITIONAL INFORMATION

Energy	Fat	Carbohydrates	Protein	Sodium
88 calories	0.4 g	20.4 g	0.8 g	7 mg

APPLE PEACH AND LEMON MOCKTAIL

Preparation Time	Total Time	Yield
5 minutes	5 minutes	4 servings

INGREDIENTS

- 2 cups (480 ml) apple juice
- 1 1/2 cups (360 ml) cold water
- 1/3 cup (80 ml) lemon juice
- 1/4 cup (60 ml) agave nectar or simple sugar syrup
- 1 medium (150 g) apple, cored and diced
- 1 medium (150 g) peach, peeled, stoned and diced
- 1 medium (70 g) lemon, cut into thin rounds
- Ice cubes, to serve
- Mint sprigs, for garnish

METHOD

- Combine the apple juice, water, lemon juice, and agave nectar in a pitcher.
- Add the apple, peach, and lemon slices. Mix well.
- Pour in serving glasses with ice cubes. Garnish with mint sprigs.
- Serve immediately and enjoy.

NUTRITIONAL INFORMATION

Energy	Fat	Carbohydrates	Protein	Sodium
122 calories	0.4 g	31.1 g	1.0 g	6 mg

SPARKLING PEACH AND LIME MOCKTAIL

Preparation Time	Total Time	Yield
5 minutes	5 minutes	4 servings

INGREDIENTS

- 1 medium (70 g) lime, cut into thin rounds
- 2 medium (300 g) peaches, peeled and diced
- 3 cups (720 ml) sparkling water
- 1/2 cup (120 ml) lime juice
- 1/3 cup (80 ml) simple sugar syrup
- Ice cubes, to serve
- Fresh rosemary sprigs, for garnish
- Peach slices, for garnish

METHOD

- Place the lime and peaches in a sturdy pitcher. Crush them using a muddler to release the juice and oil from the lime.
- Stir in sparkling water, lime juice, and sugar syrup. Mix well.
- Pour in serving glasses with ice cubes. Garnish with rosemary sprigs and peach slices.
- Serve immediately and enjoy.

NUTRITIONAL INFORMATION

Energy	Fat	Carbohydrates	Protein	Sodium
104 calories	0.5 g	26.1g	1.1 g	9 mg

STRAWBERRY ROSE AND LIME MOCKTAIL

Preparation Time	Total Time	Yield
15 minutes	15 minutes	4 servings

INGREDIENTS

- 2 cups (480 ml) boiling water
- 2 ounces (60 g) edible red rose petals
- 2 cups (400 g) fresh strawberries
- 1/4 cup (60 ml) lime juice
- 1/3 cup (80 ml) grenadine syrup
- Crushed iced, to serve
- Fresh mint sprigs, for garnish
- Chopped strawberries, for garnish

METHOD

- In a teapot, combine the boiling water and rose petals. Cover with a lid and let it steep for about 10 to 12 minutes. Strain and transfer to a sturdy pitcher.
- Add the strawberries and crush them to extract the juice using a muddler.
- Stir in lime juice and grenadine syrup. Mix well.
- Pour in serving glasses half-filled with crushed ice. Garnish with chopped strawberries and mint sprigs.
- Serve immediately and enjoy.

NUTRITIONAL INFORMATION

Energy	Fat	Carbohydrates	Protein	Sodium
308 calories	11.5 g	48.3 g	5.8 g	96 mg

ICED LAVENDER LEMONADE

Preparation Time	Total Time	Yield
15 minutes	15 minutes	4 servings

INGREDIENTS

- 2 cups (480 ml) boiling water
- 1/2 cup (30 g) lavender flowers
- 2 cups (480 ml) cold water
- 1/2 cup (120 ml) lemon juice
- 1/3 cup (80 ml) simple sugar syrup
- Ice cubes, to serve
- Lemon wedges, for garnish
- Lavender sprigs, for garnish

METHOD

- Combine the boiling water and lavender flowers in a teapot. Cover with a lid and let it steep for about 10 to 12 minutes. Strain and transfer to a pitcher.
- Stir in cold water, lemon juice, and sugar syrup. Mix well.
- Pour in serving glasses with ice cubes. Garnish with lemon wedges and lavender sprigs.
- Serve immediately and enjoy.

NUTRITIONAL INFORMATION

Energy	Fat	Carbohydrates	Protein	Sodium
70 calories	0.2 g	17.3 g	0.2 g	6 mg

FRESH LEMONADE
WITH HONEY

Preparation Time	Total Time	Yield
5 minutes	5 minutes	4 servings

INGREDIENTS

- 1 medium (85 g) lemon, cut into thin rounds
- 4 cups (960 ml) cold water
- 1/2 cup (120 ml) lemon juice
- 1/4 cup (80 ml) honey
- Ice cubes, to serve

METHOD

- Place the lemon slices and 2 cups of water in a sturdy pitcher. Crush the lemon using a muddler to release the juice and oil.
- Add the remaining water, lemon juice, and honey. Mix well.
- Pour in serving glasses with ice cubes.
- Serve immediately and enjoy.

NUTRITIONAL INFORMATION

Energy	Fat	Carbohydrates	Protein	Sodium
99 calories	0.1 g	27.3 g	0.6 g	2 mg

PINK ROSE LEMONADE

Preparation Time	Total Time	Yield
5 minutes	5 minutes	4 servings

INGREDIENTS

- 2 cups (480 ml) boiling water
- 2 ounces (60 g) edible pink rose petals
- 1 medium (85 g) lemon, cut into thin rounds
- 2 cups (480 ml) cold water
- 1/2 cup (120 ml) lemon juice
- 1/3 cup (80 ml) simple sugar syrup
- Ice cubes, to serve

METHOD

- In a teapot, combine the boiling water and rose petals. Cover with a lid and let it steep for about 10 to 12 minutes. Strain and transfer to a sturdy pitcher.
- Add the lemon slices and crush them to extract the juice and oil using a muddler.
- Stir in cold water, lemon juice, and sugar syrup. Mix well.
- Pour in serving glasses with ice cubes.
- Serve immediately and enjoy.

NUTRITIONAL INFORMATION

Energy	Fat	Carbohydrates	Protein	Sodium
76 calories	0.3 g	19.3 g	0.5 g	7 mg

FRESH LEMONADE WITH CHIA

Preparation Time	Total Time	Yield
5 minutes	5 minutes	4 servings

INGREDIENTS

- 1 medium (85 g) lemon, cut into thin rounds
- 4 cups (480 ml) cold water
- 2/3 cup (160 ml) lemon juice
- 1/3 cup (80 ml) simple sugar syrup
- 2 ounces (60 g) chia seeds
- Ice cubes, to serve

METHOD

- Place the lemon slices and 2 cups of water in a sturdy pitcher. Crush the lemon using a muddler to release the juice and oil.
- Add the remaining water, lemon juice, sugar syrup, and chia seeds. Mix well.
- Pour in serving glasses with ice cubes.
- Serve immediately and enjoy.

NUTRITIONAL INFORMATION

Energy	Fat	Carbohydrates	Protein	Sodium
118 calories	5.3 g	21.1 g	3.5 g	7 mg

SPARKLING STRAWBERRY LIMEADE

Preparation Time	Total Time	Yield
5 minutes	5 minutes	4 servings

INGREDIENTS

- 4 cups (800 g) fresh strawberries, hulled
- 1 medium lime (about 70 g), peeled and cut into small pieces
- 16 fl. oz. (480 ml) sparkling water
- 1/3 cup (80 ml) maple syrup
- Ice cubes, to serve

METHOD

- Place the strawberries and lime in a juicer. Process. Transfer juice to a pitcher.
- Stir in sparkling water and maple syrup.
- Pour in serving glasses with ice cubes.
- Serve immediately and enjoy.

NUTRITIONAL INFORMATION

Energy	Fat	Carbohydrates	Protein	Sodium
108 calories	0.5 g	25.1 g	1.1 g	3 mg

EASY KIWI LIMEADE

Preparation Time	Total Time	Yield
5 minutes	5 minutes	4 servings

INGREDIENTS

- 8 medium kiwi fruit (about 80 g each), peeled and cut into small pieces
- 1 medium lime (about 70 g), peeled and cut into small pieces
- 32 fl. oz. (960 ml) sparkling water
- 1/3 cup (80 ml) simple sugar syrup
- Ice cubes, to serve
- Kiwi and lime slices, for garnish
- Mint sprigs, for garnish

METHOD

- Place the kiwi fruit and lime in a fruit juicer. Process. Transfer juice into a pitcher.
- Stir in sparkling water and sugar syrup.
- Pour in serving glasses with ice cubes. Garnish with kiwi slices and mint sprigs.
- Serve immediately and enjoy.

NUTRITIONAL INFORMATION

Energy	Fat	Carbohydrates	Protein	Sodium
145 calories	0.8 g	36.6 g	1.9 g	7 mg

BLACKBERRY AND GINGER INFUSED WATER

Preparation Time	Total Time	Yield
5 minutes	5 minutes	4 servings

INGREDIENTS

- 2 cups (280 g) fresh blackberries
- 1 tablespoon (10 g) fresh ginger, thinly sliced
- 24 fl. oz. (720 ml) water
- Ice cubes, to serve
- Mint sprigs, for garnish

METHOD

- Place the blackberries and ginger in a pitcher with lid.
- Stir in water. Cover with a lid and let the flavors of the blackberries and ginger infuse into the water for at least 4 hours inside the fridge.
- Pour the infused water with blackberries in serving glasses with ice cubes. Garnish with mint sprigs.
- Serve and enjoy.

NUTRITIONAL INFORMATION

Energy	Fat	Carbohydrates	Protein	Sodium
46 calories	0.5 g	10.5 g	1.5 g	1 mg

RASPBERRY AND LEMON INFUSED WATER

Preparation Time	Total Time	Yield
5 minutes	5 minutes	4 servings

INGREDIENTS

- 2 cups (375 g) fresh raspberries, chopped
- 1 medium (85 g) lemon, thinly sliced into rounds
- 24 fl. oz. (720 ml) cold water
- Ice cubes, to serve

METHOD

- Place the raspberries and lemon slices in a pitcher with lid.
- Stir in water. Cover with a lid and let the flavors of the raspberries and lemon infuse into the water for at least 4 hours inside the fridge.
- Pour the infused water with fruits in serving glasses with ice cubes.
- Serve immediately and enjoy.

NUTRITIONAL INFORMATION

Energy	Fat	Carbohydrates	Protein	Sodium
38 calories	0.5 g	9.3 g	1.0 g	1 mg

LEMON AND MINT INFUSED WATER

Preparation Time	Total Time	Yield
5 minutes	5 minutes	4 servings

INGREDIENTS

- 2 medium lemon (about 85 g each), thinly sliced into rounds
- 1/2 cup (30 g) spearmint leaves
- 36 fl. oz. (960 ml) water
- Ice cubes, to serve

METHOD

- Place the lemon slices and spearmint leaves in a pitcher with lid.
- Stir in water. Cover with a lid and let the flavors of the lemon and mint infuse into the water for at least 4 hours inside the fridge.
- Pour the infused water with lemon slices and mint leaves in serving glasses with ice cubes.
- Serve immediately and enjoy.

NUTRITIONAL INFORMATION

Energy	Fat	Carbohydrates	Protein	Sodium
12 calories	0.1 g	3.9 g	0.5 g	3 mg

STRAWBERRY AND MINT INFUSED WATER

Preparation Time	Total Time	Yield
5 minutes	5 minutes	4 servings

INGREDIENTS

- 2 cups (400 g) fresh strawberries, hulled and quartered
- 1/2 cup (30 g) spearmint leaves
- 24 fl. oz. (720 ml) water
- Ice cubes, to serve

METHOD

- Place the strawberries and mint leaves in a pitcher with lid.
- Stir in water. Cover with a lid and let the flavors of the strawberries and mint infuse into the water for at least 4 hours inside the fridge.
- Pour the infused water with strawberries and mint leaves in serving glasses with ice cubes.
- Serve immediately and enjoy.

NUTRITIONAL INFORMATION

Energy	Fat	Carbohydrates	Protein	Sodium
23 calories	0.2 g	5.5 g	0.5 g	1 mg

PINK ROSE AND LEMON INFUSED WATER

Preparation Time	Total Time	Yield
5 minutes	5 minutes	4 servings

INGREDIENTS

- 2 ounces (60 g) edible pink rose petals
- 2 medium lemon (about 85 g each), cut into wedges
- 32 fl. oz. (960 ml) water
- Ice cubes, to serve

METHOD

- Place the rose petals and lemon wedges in a pitcher with lid.
- Stir in water. Cover with a lid and let the flavors of the pink rose and lemon infuse into the water for at least 4 hours inside the fridge.
- Pour the infused water with rose petals and lemon wedges in serving glasses with ice cubes.
- Serve immediately and enjoy.

NUTRITIONAL INFORMATION

Energy	Fat	Carbohydrates	Protein	Sodium
12 calories	0.1 g	3.9 g	0.5 g	1 mg

CUCUMBER LEMON LIME SODA

Preparation Time	Total Time	Yield
5 minutes	5 minutes	4 servings

INGREDIENTS

- 1 medium (200 g) cucumber, thinly sliced into rounds
- 32 fl. oz. (960 ml) lemon lime soda
- Ice cubes, to serve
- Mint sprigs, for garnish

METHOD

- Divide the cucumber slices among 4 serving glasses with ice cubes.
- Pour the lemon lime soda. Garnish with mint sprigs.
- Serve immediately and enjoy.

NUTRITIONAL INFORMATION

Energy	Fat	Carbohydrates	Protein	Sodium
111 calories	0.1 g	29.9 g	0.5 g	52 mg

MINTY STRAWBERRY LEMON LIME SODA

Preparation Time	Total Time	Yield
5 minutes	5 minutes	4 servings

INGREDIENTS

- 2 cups (400 g) fresh strawberries, hulled and chopped
- 1/2 cup (30 g) spearmint leaves
- 24 fl. oz. (720 ml) lemon lime soda
- Ice cubes, to serve

METHOD

- Divide the strawberries and mint leaves among 4 serving glasses with ice cubes.
- Pour the lemon lime soda.
- Serve immediately and enjoy.

NUTRITIONAL INFORMATION

Energy	Fat	Carbohydrates	Protein	Sodium
98 calories	0.2 g	25.9 g	0.5 g	15 mg

ICED ORANGE LEMON AND HONEY

Preparation Time	Total Time	Yield
5 minutes	5 minutes	4 servings

INGREDIENTS

- 2 cups (480 ml) freshly squeezed orange juice
- 2 cups (480 ml) sparkling water
- 1/2 cup (120 ml) lemon juice
- 1/4 cup (80 ml) honey
- Ice cubes, to serve
- Orange slices, for garnish

METHOD

- Combine the orange juice, sparkling water, lemon juice, and honey in a pitcher. Mix well.
- Pour in juice glasses with ice cubes. Garnish with orange slices.
- Serve immediately and enjoy.

NUTRITIONAL INFORMATION

Energy	Fat	Carbohydrates	Protein	Sodium
156 calories	0.6 g	37.5 g	1.6 g	8 mg

GRAPEFRUIT COOLER WITH ROSEMARY

Preparation Time	Total Time	Yield
5 minutes	5 minutes	4 servings

INGREDIENTS

- 1 medium (250 g) grapefruit, juiced
- 1 medium (70 g) lime, juiced
- 3 cups (240 ml) sparkling water
- 1/3 cup (80 ml) simple sugar syrup
- 4 fresh rosemary sprigs
- Ice cubes, to serve
- Grapefruit wedges, for garnish
- Rosemary sprigs, for garnish

METHOD

- Combine the grapefruit juice, lime juice, sparkling water, sugar syrup, and rosemary sprigs in a pitcher.
- Pour in serving glasses with ice cubes. Garnish with grapefruit wedges and rosemary sprigs.
- Serve immediately and enjoy.

NUTRITIONAL INFORMATION

Energy	Fat	Carbohydrates	Protein	Sodium
70 calories	0.1 g	18.7 g	0.5 g	2 mg

ORANGE AND APPLE COOLER WITH MINT

Preparation Time	Total Time	Yield
5 minutes	5 minutes	4 servings

INGREDIENTS

- 2 cups (480 ml) fresh orange juice
- 1 cup (240 ml) apple juice
- 1 cup (240 ml) sparkling water
- 1/4 cup (80 ml) honey
- 1 medium orange, cut into wedges
- 1/2 cup fresh spearmint leaves
- 1 ½ cups (375 g) ice cubes

METHOD

- Combine the orange juice, apple juice, honey, and sparkling water in a pitcher. Mix well.
- Add the orange wedges, mint leaves, and ice cubes. Mix well.
- Pour in serving glasses.
- Serve immediately and enjoy.

NUTRITIONAL INFORMATION

Energy	Fat	Carbohydrates	Protein	Sodium
149 calories	0.3 g	37.0g	1.0 g	5 mg

SPARKLING WATERMELON AND STRAWBERRY COOLER

Preparation Time	Total Time	Yield
5 minutes	5 minutes	4 servings

INGREDIENTS

- 3 cups (450 g) watermelon, cubed
- 2 cups (400 g) strawberries, halved
- 16 fl. oz. (480 ml) sparkling water
- 1/4 cup (60 ml) lime juice
- 1/3 cup (80 ml) simple sugar syrup
- Ice cubes, to serve
- Mint sprigs, to serve

METHOD

- Place the watermelon and strawberry in a fruit juicer. Process. Transfer juice into a pitcher.
- Stir in sparkling water, lime juice, and sugar syrup.
- Pour in serving glasses with ice cubes. Garnish with watermelon slices and mint sprigs.
- Serve immediately and enjoy.

NUTRITIONAL INFORMATION

Energy	Fat	Carbohydrates	Protein	Sodium
108 calories	0.5 g	26.9 g	1.3 g	6 mg

PINEAPPLE LEMON COOLER WITH MINT

Preparation Time	Total Time	Yield
5 minutes	5 minutes	4 servings

INGREDIENTS

- 2 cups (480 ml) pineapple juice
- 2 cups (480 ml) cold water
- 1/2 cup (120 ml) lemon juice
- 1/4 cup (80 ml) honey
- 1 handful fresh mint leaves
- Ice cubes, to serve
- Lemon wedges, for garnish

METHOD

- Combine the pineapple juice, water, lemon juice, and honey in a pitcher. Mix well.
- Stir in fresh mint leaves.
- Pour in serving glasses with ice cubes. Garnish with lemon wedges.
- Serve immediately and enjoy.

NUTRITIONAL INFORMATION

Energy	Fat	Carbohydrates	Protein	Sodium
138 calories	0.4 g	34.9 g	0.8 g	0.8 mg

TROPICAL CITRUS COOLER

Preparation Time	Total Time	Yield
5 minutes	5 minutes	4 servings

INGREDIENTS

- 2 cups (480 ml) coconut water
- 1 cup (240 ml) pineapple juice
- 1 cup (240 ml) orange juice
- 1/4 cup (60 ml) lime juice
- 1/3 cup (80 ml) simple sugar syrup
- Ice cubes, to serve
- Fresh mint sprigs

METHOD

- Combine the coconut water, pineapple juice, orange juice, lime juice, and sugar syrup in a pitcher. Mix well.
- Pour in juice glasses with ice cubes. Garnish with orange slices and mint sprigs.
- Serve immediately and enjoy.

NUTRITIONAL INFORMATION

Energy	Fat	Carbohydrates	Protein	Sodium
150 calories	0.6 g	35.9 g	1.6 g	131 mg

MANGO AND LIME COOLER

Preparation Time	Total Time	Yield
5 minutes	5 minutes	4 servings

INGREDIENTS

- 4 cups (660 g) mango, diced
- 1 medium (70 g) lime, cut into small pieces
- 2 cups (480 ml) cold water
- 1/4 cup (80 ml) honey
- Ice cubes, to serve

METHOD

- Place the mangoes and lime in a fruit juicer. Process. Transfer juice into a pitcher.
- Stir in cold water and honey.
- Pour juice in serving glasses with ice cubes.
- Serve immediately and enjoy.

NUTRITIONAL INFORMATION

Energy	Fat	Carbohydrates	Protein	Sodium
143 calories	0.5 g	37.4 g	1.2 g	2 mg

WATERMELON LIME COOLER WITH AGAVE

Preparation Time	Total Time	Yield
5 minutes	5 minutes	4 servings

INGREDIENTS

- 6 cups (900 g) watermelon, seedless
- 1 medium (70 g) lime, juiced
- 1 cup (240 ml) cold water
- 1/4 cup (60 ml) agave nectar
- Crushed ice, to serve

METHOD

- Place the watermelon, juice of 1 lime, water, and agave nectar in a blender. Process.
- Strain using a fine sieve or strainer. Pour juice in serving glasses half-filled with crushed ice.
- Serve immediately and enjoy.

NUTRITIONAL INFORMATION

Energy	Fat	Carbohydrates	Protein	Sodium
130 calories	0.4 g	32.7 g	2.3 g	14 mg

CITRUS AND HERB COOLER

Preparation Time	Total Time	Yield
5 minutes	5 minutes	4 servings

INGREDIENTS

- 6 medium fresh oranges (about 150 g each), juiced
- Juice of one lime
- 2 cups (480 ml) cold water
- 1 handful of sweet basil
- Honey, to taste
- Ice cubes, to serve
- Orange and lime wedges, for garnish

METHOD

- Combine the freshly-squeezed orange juice, lime juice, water, and basil in a jug or pitcher. Drizzle some honey to taste. Stir.
- Pour in serving glasses over ice cubes.
- Garnish with orange and lime wedges.
- Serve immediately and enjoy.

NUTRITIONAL INFORMATION

Energy	Fat	Carbohydrates	Protein	Sodium
129 calories	0.3 g	33.5 g	2.0 g	1 mg

CITRUS PINEAPPLE COOLER

Preparation Time	Total Time	Yield
5 minutes	5 minutes	4 servings

INGREDIENTS

- 4 cups (660 g) pineapple, cubed
- 2 medium orange (about 150 g each), peeled and cut into small pieces
- 1 medium (85g) lemon, peeled and cut into small pieces
- Honey, to taste
- Crushed ice, to serve

METHOD

- Place the pineapple, orange, and lemon in a juicer. Process.
- Pour juice in serving glasses with some crushed ice. Add some honey to taste.
- Serve immediately and enjoy.

NUTRITIONAL INFORMATION

Energy	Fat	Carbohydrates	Protein	Sodium
135 calories	0.3 g	35.6 g	1.8 g	3 mg

MINTY PINEAPPLE AND LEMON COOLER

Preparation Time	Total Time	Yield
5 minutes	5 minutes	4 servings

INGREDIENTS

- 2 cups (500 ml) pineapple juice, unsweetened
- 1/4 cup (60 ml) lemon juice
- 1/4 cup (60 ml) lime juice
- 16 fl. oz. (480 ml) cold water
- 1/2 cup (30 g) fresh mint leaves
- Honey, to taste
- Ice cubes, to serve
- Lemon and lime slices, for garnish

METHOD

- Combine the pineapple juice, lemon juice, lime juice, water, and mint leaves in a pitcher. Add some honey to taste. Stir until blended well.
- Pour in serving glasses over ice cubes.
- Garnish with mint sprigs and slices of lemon, lime and pineapple.
- Serve immediately and enjoy.

NUTRITIONAL INFORMATION

Energy	Fat	Carbohydrates	Protein	Sodium
105 calories	0.0 g	25.4 g	0.7 g	9 mg

CRANBERRY ORANGE AND LIME COOLER

Preparation Time	Total Time	Yield
5 minutes	5 minutes	4 servings

INGREDIENTS

- 16 fl. oz. (480 ml) cranberry juice
- 8 fl. oz. (240 ml) orange juice
- 2 fl. oz. (60 ml) lime juice
- 8 fl. oz. (240 ml) sparkling water
- 1/3 cup (80 ml) simple sugar syrup
- Ice cubes, to serve
- Orange and lime slices, for garnish

METHOD

- Combine the cranberry juice, orange juice, and lime juice in a pitcher.
- Stir in sparkling water and sugar syrup. Mix until blended well.
- Pour in tall glasses with ice cubes. Garnish with orange and lime slices.
- Serve immediately and enjoy.

NUTRITIONAL INFORMATION

Energy	Fat	Carbohydrates	Protein	Sodium
124 calories	0.3 g	28.4 g	0.5 g	4 mg

CHERRY AND RED GRAPE COOLER

Preparation Time	Total Time	Yield
5 minutes	5 minutes	4 servings

INGREDIENTS

- 16 fl. oz. (480 ml) tart cherry juice
- 16 fl. oz. (480 ml) sparkling red grape juice
- Grenadine syrup, to taste (optional)
- Ice cubes, to serve
- Fresh cherries, for garnish (optional)

METHOD

- Combine the cherry juice, and red grape juice in a pitcher. Drizzle with some grenadine syrup to taste. Mix well.
- Pour in tall glasses with ice cubes. Garnish with fresh cherries if desired.
- Serve immediately and enjoy.

NUTRITIONAL INFORMATION

Energy	Fat	Carbohydrates	Protein	Sodium
140 calories	0.0 g	35.0 g	0.0 g	32 mg

PAPAYA AND LIME COOLER WITH HONEY

Preparation Time	Total Time	Yield
5 minutes	5 minutes	4 servings

INGREDIENTS

- 4 cups (560 g) papaya, cubed
- 1 medium (70 g) lime, quartered
- 16 fl. oz. (480 ml) cold water
- 1/4 cup (80 ml) honey
- Crushed ice, to serve
- Mint sprigs, for garnish

METHOD

- Place the papaya and lime in a juicer. Process. Transfer juice to a pitcher.
- Stir in water and honey. Mix until blended well.
- Pour in serving glasses half-filled with crushed ice. Garnish with mint sprigs.
- Serve immediately and enjoy.

NUTRITIONAL INFORMATION

Energy	Fat	Carbohydrates	Protein	Sodium
131 calories	0.4 g	34.9 g	0.9 g	13 mg

ICED POMEGRANATE TEA WITH MAPLE

Preparation Time	Total Time	Yield
5 minutes	5 minutes	4 servings

INGREDIENTS

- 16 fl. oz. (480 ml) freshly brewed hibiscus tea, cooled
- 16 fl. oz. (480 ml) pomegranate juice
- 1/4 cup (80 ml) maple syrup
- Ice cubes, to serve
- Mint sprigs, for garnish

METHOD

- Combine the hisbiscus tea, pomegranate juice, and sugar syrup in a pitcher. Stir.
- Pour in serving glasses with ice cubes. Garnish with mint sprigs.
- Serve immediately and enjoy.

NUTRITIONAL INFORMATION

Energy	Fat	Carbohydrates	Protein	Sodium
139 calories	0.1 g	34.1 g	0.5 g	10 mg

ICED FRUITY HIBISCUS TEA

Preparation Time	Total Time	Yield
5 minutes	5 minutes	4 servings

INGREDIENTS

- 2 hibiscus tea bags
- 2 cups (480 ml) boiling water
- 1 cup (240 ml) cranberry juice
- Juice of 1/2 lemon
- Juice of 1/2 lime
- 1 cup (200 g) fresh strawberries, quartered
- Maple syrup, to taste
- Ice cubes, to serve
- Lemon and lime slices, to serve

METHOD

- Steep the hibiscus tea bags in boiling water for 5 minutes. Transfer to a pitcher.
- Add the cranberry juice, lemon juice, and lime juice. Drizzle some maple syrup to taste.
- Add the strawberries as well as the lemon and lime slices. Mix well.
- Pour in serving glasses over ice cubes.
- Serve immediately and enjoy.

NUTRITIONAL INFORMATION

Energy	Fat	Carbohydrates	Protein	Sodium
86 calories	0.2 g	19.7 g	0.4 g	2 mg

ICED BLACK TEA WITH LEMON

Preparation Time	Total Time	Yield
5 minutes	5 minutes	4 servings

INGREDIENTS

- 4 cups (960 ml) freshly brewed black tea, cooled
- 1/2 cup (120 ml) lemon juice
- 1/4 cup (80 ml) honey
- Ice cubes, to serve
- Lemon slices, for garnish

METHOD

- Combine the brewed tea, lemon juice, and honey in a pitcher. Mix well.
- Pour in tall glasses with ice cubes. Garnish with lemon slices.
- Serve immediately and enjoy.

NUTRITIONAL INFORMATION

Energy	Fat	Carbohydrates	Protein	Sodium
72 calories	0.2 g	18.2 g	0.3 g	7 mg

FIG AND GINGER ICED TEA WITH THYME

Preparation Time	Total Time	Yield
5 minutes	5 minutes	4 servings

INGREDIENTS

- 3 cups (720 ml) freshly brewed ginger tea, cooled
- 4 medium figs (about 70 g each), cut into small pieces
- 4 fresh thyme sprigs
- Ice cubes, to serve
- Fig halves, to serve

METHOD

- Combine the ginger tea and figs in a sturdy pitcher. Crush the figs using a muddler to release the juice and flavor.
- Stir in thyme sprigs. Mix well.
- Pour in serving glasses with ice cubes and fig halves.
- Serve immediately and enjoy.

NUTRITIONAL INFORMATION

Energy	Fat	Carbohydrates	Protein	Sodium
69 calories	0.5 g	17.0 g	0.9 g	2 mg

ICED GINGER AND LIME TEA WITH HONEY

Preparation Time	Total Time	Yield
5 minutes	5 minutes	4 servings

INGREDIENTS

- 4 cups (960 ml) freshly brewed ginger tea, cooled
- 1/2 cup (120 ml) lime juice
- 1/4 cup (80 ml) honey
- Ice cubes, to serve
- Lime slices, for garnish
- Fresh mint sprigs, for garnish

METHOD

- Combine the ginger tea, lime juice, and honey in a pitcher. Mix well.
- Pour in serving glasses with ice cubes. Garnish with lime slices.
- Serve immediately and enjoy.

NUTRITIONAL INFORMATION

Energy	Fat	Carbohydrates	Protein	Sodium
85 calories	0.5 g	20.8 g	0.6 g	8 mg

ICED ORANGE TURMERIC TEA

Preparation Time	Total Time	Yield
5 minutes	5 minutes	4 servings

INGREDIENTS

- 3 cups (720 ml) freshly brewed turmeric tea, cooled
- 1 cup (240 ml) orange juice
- 1/4 cup (80 ml) honey
- Ice cubes, to serve
- Orange slices, for garnish

METHOD

- Combine the turmeric tea, orange juice, and honey in a pitcher. Mix well.
- Pour in tall glasses with ice cubes. Garnish with orange slices.
- Serve immediately and enjoy.

NUTRITIONAL INFORMATION

Energy	Fat	Carbohydrates	Protein	Sodium
106 calories	0.5 g	26.3 g	0.8 g	3 mg

CRANBERRY ICED TEA WITH MINT

Preparation Time	Total Time	Yield
5 minutes	5 minutes	4 servings

INGREDIENTS

- 2 ½ cups (600 ml) freshly brewed hibiscus tea, cooled
- 1 ½ cups (360 ml) cranberry juice
- 1 ounce (30 g) fresh spearmint leaves
- 1/4 cup (80 ml) maple syrup
- Ice cubes, to serve
- Mint sprigs, for garnish
- Fresh cranberries, for garnish

METHOD

- Combine the hibiscus tea, cranberry juice, spearmint, and maple syrup in a pitcher. Mix well.
- Pour in serving glasses with ice cubes. Garnish with cranberries and mint sprigs.
- Serve immediately and enjoy.

NUTRITIONAL INFORMATION

Energy	Fat	Carbohydrates	Protein	Sodium
74 calories	0.3 g	17.3 g	0.0 g	2 mg

ICED PINEAPPLE AND YELLOW TEA

Preparation Time	Total Time	Yield
5 minutes	5 minutes	4 servings

INGREDIENTS

- 2 ½ cups (600 ml) freshly brewed yellow tea, cooled
- 1 ½ cups (360 ml) pineapple juice
- 1/4 cup (80 ml) honey
- Ice cubes, to serve

METHOD

- Combine the yellow tea, pineapple juice, and honey in a pitcher. Mix well.
- Pour in serving glasses with ice cubes.
- Serve immediately and enjoy.

NUTRITIONAL INFORMATION

Energy	Fat	Carbohydrates	Protein	Sodium
116 calories	0.1 g	30.0 g	0.4 g	7 mg

CITRUS ICED TEA WITH BASIL

Preparation Time	Total Time	Yield
5 minutes	5 minutes	4 servings

INGREDIENTS

- 3 cups (720 ml) freshly brewed hibiscus tea, cooled
- 1 cup (240 ml) fresh orange juice
- 1/4 cup (60 ml) lemon juice
- 1/4 cup (80 ml) honey
- 1/4 cup (15 g) fresh basil leaves
- Ice cubes, to serve
- Basil sprigs, for garnish
- Lemon wedges, for garnish

METHOD

- Combine the hibiscus tea, orange juice, lemon juice, honey, and basil leaves in a pitcher. Mix well.
- Pour in serving glasses with ice cubes. Garnish with lemon wedges and basil sprigs.
- Serve immediately and enjoy.

NUTRITIONAL INFORMATION

Energy	Fat	Carbohydrates	Protein	Sodium
98 calories	0.3 g	24.8 g	0.7 g	10 mg

ICED OOLONG TEA WITH LIME

Preparation Time	Total Time	Yield
5 minutes	5 minutes	4 servings

INGREDIENTS

- 4 cups (960 ml) freshly brewed oolong tea, cooled
- 1/2 cup (120 ml) lime juice
- 1/4 cup (80 ml) agave nectar
- Ice cubes, to serve
- Lime wedges, to serve
- Mint sprigs, for garnish

METHOD

- Combine the oolong tea, lime juice, and agave nectar in a pitcher. Mix well.
- Pour in serving glasses with ice cubes and lime wedges. Garnish with mint sprigs.
- Serve immediately and enjoy.

NUTRITIONAL INFORMATION

Energy	Fat	Carbohydrates	Protein	Sodium
60 calories	0.0 g	16.0 g	0.0 g	0 mg

STRAWBERRY ICED TEA

Preparation Time	Total Time	Yield
5 minutes	5 minutes	4 servings

INGREDIENTS

- 3 cups (720 ml) freshly brewed yellow tea, cooled
- 2 cups (400 g) strawberries, hulled
- 1/4 cup (60 ml) lemon juice
- 1/3 cup (80 ml) simple sugar syrup
- Ice cubes, to serve
- Strawberry slices, to serve
- Mint sprigs, for garnish

METHOD

- Place the strawberries in your juicer. Process. Transfer juice to a pitcher.
- Stir in brewed yellow tea, lemon juice, and sugar syrup. Mix well.
- Pour in serving glasses with ice cubes and strawberry slices. Garnish with mint sprigs.
- Serve immediately and enjoy.

NUTRITIONAL INFORMATION

Energy	Fat	Carbohydrates	Protein	Sodium
89 calories	0.3 g	22.5 g	0.6 g	4 mg

ICED HONEY LEMON TEA

Preparation Time	Total Time	Yield
3 minutes	3 minutes	2 servings

INGREDIENTS

- 32 fl. oz. (960 ml) freshly brewed black tea, cooled
- 3 fl. oz. (90 ml) lemon juice
- 1/4 cup (80 ml) honey
- Ice cubes, to serve
- Lemon slices, for garnish
- Mint sprigs, for garnish

METHOD

- Combine the freshly brewed tea, lemon juice, and honey in a pitcher. Stir.
- Pour in serving glasses over ice cubes. Garnish with lemon slices and mint sprigs.
- Serve immediately and enjoy.

NUTRITIONAL INFORMATION

Energy	Fat	Carbohydrates	Protein	Sodium
71 calories	0.1 g	19.6 g	0.2 g	1 mg

WATERMELON CUCUMBER SLUSHY

Preparation Time	Total Time	Yield
5 minutes	5 minutes	4 servings

INGREDIENTS

- 4 cups (600 g) seedless watermelon, cut into small pieces
- 1 medium (200 g) cucumber, cut into small pieces
- 1/3 cup (80 ml) simple sugar syrup
- Crushed ice, to serve
- Mint sprigs, for garnish

METHOD

- Combine the watermelon, cucumber, and sugar syrup in a blender. Process until smooth.
- Pour in tall glasses half-filled with crushed ice. Garnish with mint sprigs.
- Serve immediately and enjoy.

NUTRITIONAL INFORMATION

Energy	Fat	Carbohydrates	Protein	Sodium
104 calories	0.3 g	26.7 g	1.4 g	4 mg

COCO MELON SLUSHY

Preparation Time	Total Time	Yield
5 minutes	5 minutes	4 servings

INGREDIENTS

- 4 cups (680 g) frozen melon, cubed
- 2 cups (480 ml) coconut water
- 1/4 cup (80 ml) honey
- Melon slices, for garnish

METHOD

- Place the frozen melon, coconut water, and honey in a blender. Process.
- Pour in individual glasses. Garnish with melon slices.
- Serve immediately and enjoy.

NUTRITIONAL INFORMATION

Energy	Fat	Carbohydrates	Protein	Sodium
108 calories	0.5 g	25.8 g	2.2 g	151 mg

MANGO PEACH SLUSHY

Preparation Time	Total Time	Yield
5 minutes	5 minutes	4 servings

INGREDIENTS

- 2 cups (330 g) mango, diced
- 2 cups (300 g) peach, diced
- 1/4 cup (60 ml) lemon juice
- 1 cup (240 ml) water
- 1/4 cup (60 ml) simple sugar syrup
- 2 cups (500 g) ice cubes
- Mango and peach slices, for garnish

METHOD

- Combine the mango, peach, lemon juice, water, sugar syrup, and ice cubes in a blender. Process until smooth.
- Pour in serving glasses. Garnish with mango and peach slices.
- Serve immediately and enjoy.

NUTRITIONAL INFORMATION

Energy	Fat	Carbohydrates	Protein	Sodium
130 calories	0.6 g	32.2 g	1.5 g	6 mg

RED CURRANT CHERRY AND STRAWBERRY SLUSHY

Preparation Time	Total Time	Yield
5 minutes	5 minutes	4 servings

INGREDIENTS

- 1 cup (200 g) strawberries, hulled and halved
- 1 cup (120 g) red currants
- 1 cup (150 g) cherries, pitted
- 1 cup (240 ml) water
- 1/4 cup (60 ml) lemon juice
- 1/4 cup (60 ml) simple sugar syrup
- 2 cups (500 g) ice cubes
- Red currants, for garnish
- Strawberry slices, for garnish

METHOD

- Combine the strawberries, currants, cherries, water, lemon juice, sugar syrup, and ice cubes in a blender. Process until smooth.
- Pour in serving glasses. Garnish with currants and strawberry slices.
- Serve immediately and enjoy.

NUTRITIONAL INFORMATION

Energy	Fat	Carbohydrates	Protein	Sodium
100 calories	0.4 g	25.2 g	1.3 g	4 mg

PAPAYA PINEAPPLE AND LIME SLUSHY

Preparation Time	Total Time	Yield
5 minutes	5 minutes	4 servings

INGREDIENTS

- 3 cups (420 g) ripe papaya, cubed
- 1 cup (240 ml) pineapple juice
- 1/2 cup (120 ml) lime juice
- 1/4 cup (60 ml) simple sugar syrup
- 1 ½ cups (375 g) ice cubes
- Lime slices, for garnish

METHOD

- Place the papaya, pineapple juice, lime juice, sugar syrup, and ice cubes in a blender. Process until smooth.
- Pour in serving glasses. Garnish with lime slices.
- Serve immediately and enjoy.

NUTRITIONAL INFORMATION

Energy	Fat	Carbohydrates	Protein	Sodium
134 calories	0.6 g	33.0 g	1.0 g	16 mg

STRAWBERRY AND POMEGRANATE SLUSHY

Preparation Time	Total Time	Yield
5 minutes	5 minutes	4 servings

INGREDIENTS

- 1 cup (200 g) strawberries, hulled and halved
- 1 cup (180 g) pomegranate seeds
- 1/4 cup (60 ml) lemon juice
- 1 cup (240 ml) water
- 1/4 cup (80 ml) maple syrup
- 2 cups (500 g) ice cubes
- Strawberries, for garnish
- Mint sprigs, for garnish

METHOD

- Combine the strawberries, pomegranate seeds, lemon juice, water, maple syrup, and ice cubes in a blender. Process until smooth.
- Pour in serving glasses. Garnish with strawberries and mint sprigs.
- Serve immediately and enjoy.

NUTRITIONAL INFORMATION

Energy	Fat	Carbohydrates	Protein	Sodium
99 calories	0.3 g	24.1 g	0.7 g	5 mg

GRAPEFRUIT SLUSHY WITH AGAVE

Preparation Time	Total Time	Yield
5 minutes	5 minutes	4 servings

INGREDIENTS

- 2 medium grapefruit (about 250 g each)
- 1 cup (240 ml) water
- 1/3 cup (80 ml) simple sugar syrup
- 2 cups (500 g) ice cubes
- Mint sprigs, for garnish

METHOD

- Peel the grapefruit, remove the seeds, and cut into segments.
- Combine the grapefruit, water, sugar syrup, and ice cubes in a blender. Process until smooth.
- Pour in serving glasses. Garnish with mint sprigs.
- Serve immediately and enjoy.

NUTRITIONAL INFORMATION

Energy	Fat	Carbohydrates	Protein	Sodium
103 calories	0.1 g	27.0 g	0.8 g	0 mg

PINEAPPLE COCONUT AND LEMON SLUSHY

Preparation Time	Total Time	Yield
5 minutes	5 minutes	4 servings

INGREDIENTS

- 4 cups (495 g) frozen pineapple, cut into cubes
- 2 cups (480 ml) coconut water
- 1/4 cup (60 ml) lemon juice
- Honey, to taste

METHOD

- Combine the frozen pineapple, coconut water, and lemon juice in a blender. Drizzle some honey to taste. Process until smooth.
- Pour in serving glasses. Garnish with pineapple slices.
- Serve immediately and enjoy.

NUTRITIONAL INFORMATION

Energy	Fat	Carbohydrates	Protein	Sodium
140 calories	0.6 g	35.1 g	1.9 g	120 mg

WATERMELON ORANGE AND PINEAPPLE SLUSHY

Preparation Time	Total Time	Yield
5 minutes	5 minutes	4 servings

INGREDIENTS

- 3 cups (450 g) watermelon, cubed
- 1 cup (240 ml) orange juice
- 1 cup (240 ml) pineapple juice
- 1 ½ cups (375 g) ice cubes
- Honey, to taste (optional)
- Watermelon slices, for garnish

METHOD

- Place the watermelon, orange juice, pineapple juice, and ice cubes in a blender. Drizzle some honey to taste. Process until smooth.
- Pour in individual glasses. Garnish with a slice of watermelon.
- Serve immediately and enjoy.

NUTRITIONAL INFORMATION

Energy	Fat	Carbohydrates	Protein	Sodium
127 calories	0.4 g	31.7 g	1.4 g	4 mg

PINEAPPLE ORANGE AND COCONUT SLUSHY

Preparation Time	Total Time	Yield
3 minutes	3 minutes	4 servings

INGREDIENTS

- 1 cup (240 ml) pineapple juice
- 1 cup (240 ml) freshly squeezed orange juice
- 1 cup (240 ml) coconut water
- 1 ½ cups (375 g) ice cubes
- Honey, to taste

METHOD

- Combine the pineapple juice, orange juice, coconut water, and ice cubes in a blender. Add some honey to taste. Process until smooth.
- Pour in serving glasses. Garnish with pineapple or orange slices if desired.
- Serve immediately and enjoy.

NUTRITIONAL INFORMATION

Energy	Fat	Carbohydrates	Protein	Sodium
145 calories	0.8 g	36.6 g	1.9 g	7 mg

These smoothie recipes are excellent thirst quenchers to beat the summer heat.

The whole family can enjoy them during your next pool party or day at the beach!

AVOCADO BANANA AND ALMOND SMOOTHIE

Preparation Time	Total Time	Yield
5 minutes	5 minutes	4 servings

INGREDIENTS

- 1 medium (200 g) avocado, cut into small pieces
- 2 medium banana (about 120 g each), cut into small pieces
- 2 cups (480 ml) almond milk
- 2 tablespoons (40 ml) honey
- 1 ½ cups (375 g) ice cubes
- Fresh mint sprigs

METHOD

- Place the avocado, banana, almond milk, honey, and ice cubes in a blender. Process until smooth.
- Pour in serving glasses. Garnish with mint sprigs.
- Serve immediately and enjoy.

NUTRITIONAL INFORMATION

Energy	Fat	Carbohydrates	Protein	Sodium
220 calories	11.2 g	27.0 g	2.1 g	79 mg

BANANA COCONUT AND LIME SMOOTHIE

Preparation Time	Total Time	Yield
5 minutes	5 minutes	4 servings

INGREDIENTS

- 2 medium banana (about 120 g each), cut into small pieces
- 2 cups (480 ml) coconut water
- 1/2 cup (120 ml) coconut milk
- 1/3 cup (80 ml) simple sugar syrup
- 1/4 cup (60 ml) lime juice
- 1 ½ cups (375 g) ice cubes
- Lime slices, for garnish

METHOD

- Place the banana, coconut water, coconut milk, sugar syrup, lime juice, and ice cubes in a blender. Process until smooth.
- Pour in serving glasses. Garnish with lime slices.
- Serve immediately and enjoy.

NUTRITIONAL INFORMATION

Energy	Fat	Carbohydrates	Protein	Sodium
195 calories	7.7 g	32.4 g	2.3 g	134 mg

BERRY ORANGE AND KIWI SMOOTHIE

Preparation Time	Total Time	Yield
5 minutes	5 minutes	4 servings

INGREDIENTS

- 2 cups (480 ml) almond milk
- 1 cup (200 g) strawberries, hulled
- 1 cup (150 g) blueberries
- 1 medium (140 g) orange, peeled and cut into segments
- 1 medium (80 g) kiwi fruit, peeled and cut into small pieces
- 1/4 cup (80 ml) honey
- 1½ cups (375 g) ice cubes
- Orange and kiwi slices, for garnish
- Strawberries and blueberries, for garnish

METHOD

- Place the almond milk, strawberries, orange, kiwi fruit, and ice cubes in a blender. Process until smooth.
- Pour in individual glasses. Garnish with fruit slices and berries.
- Serve immediately and enjoy.

NUTRITIONAL INFORMATION

Energy	Fat	Carbohydrates	Protein	Sodium
139 calories	1.6 g	32.6 g	1.6 g	77 mg

BLUEBERRY BANANA AND COCONUT SMOOTHIE

Preparation Time	Total Time	Yield
5 minutes	5 minutes	4 servings

INGREDIENTS

- 2 cups (480 ml) coconut water
- 2 cups (310 g) blueberries, frozen
- 2 medium banana (about 120 g each), cut into small pieces
- 1/2 cup (120 ml) coconut milk
- Blueberries, for garnish

METHOD

- Place the coconut water, blueberries, banana, and coconut milk in a blender. Process until smooth.
- Pour in serving glasses. Garnish with blueberries.
- Serve immediately and enjoy.

NUTRITIONAL INFORMATION

Energy	Fat	Carbohydrates	Protein	Sodium
139 calories	1.6 g	32.6 g	1.6 g	77 mg

COCONUT MELON AND BANANA SMOOTHIE

Preparation Time	Total Time	Yield
5 minutes	5 minutes	4 servings

INGREDIENTS

- 2 cups (340 g) honeydew melon, cubed
- 2 medium banana (about 120 g each), cut into small pieces
- 1 cup (240 ml) coconut water
- 1/2 cup (120 ml) coconut milk
- 1/4 cup (60 ml) simple sugar syrup
- 1 ½ cups (375 g) ice cubes
- Honeydew melon slices, for garnish

METHOD

- Place the honeydew melon, banana, coconut water, coconut milk, sugar syrup, and ice cubes in a blender. Process until smooth.
- Pour in individual glasses. Garnish with melon slices.
- Serve immediately and enjoy.

NUTRITIONAL INFORMATION

Energy	Fat	Carbohydrates	Protein	Sodium
197 calories	7.6 g	34.1 g	2.2 g	83 mg

STRAWBERRY BANANA AND COCONUT SHAKE

Preparation Time	Total Time	Yield
5 minutes	5 minutes	4 servings

INGREDIENTS

- 2 cups (440 g) frozen strawberries, hulled
- 2 medium banana (about 120 g each), sliced
- 2 cups (480 ml) coconut water
- 1/2 cup (120 ml) coconut milk
- 1/4 cup (60 ml) simple sugar syrup
- Strawberries, for garnish

METHOD

- Place the strawberries, banana, coconut water, coconut milk, and sugar syrup in a blender. Process until smooth.
- Pour in serving glasses. Garnish with strawberries.
- Serve immediately and enjoy.

NUTRITIONAL INFORMATION

Energy	Fat	Carbohydrates	Protein	Sodium
205 calories	7.8 g	35.1 g	2.7 g	132 mg

DRAGONFRUIT PLUM AND BANANA SHAKE

Preparation Time	Total Time	Yield
5 minutes	5 minutes	4 servings

INGREDIENTS

- 2 medium dragonfruit (about 200 g each), peeled and cut into small pieces
- 2 medium plum (about 70 g each), cut into small pieces
- 1 medium (120 g) banana, cut into small pieces
- 1 cup (240 ml) coconut water
- 1 ½ cups (375 g) ice cubes
- Mint sprigs, for garnish

METHOD

- Place the dragonfruit, plum, banana, coconut water, and ice cubes in a blender. Process until smooth.
- Pour in chilled serving glasses. Garnish with mint sprigs.
- Serve immediately and enjoy.

NUTRITIONAL INFORMATION

Energy	Fat	Carbohydrates	Protein	Sodium
138 calories	2.2 g	27.5 g	3.3 g	123 mg

COCO BANANA AND FLAX SMOOTHIE

Preparation Time	Total Time	Yield
5 minutes	5 minutes	4 servings

INGREDIENTS

- 2 cups (480 ml) coconut water
- 1/2 cup (120 ml) coconut milk
- 4 medium banana (about 120 g each), cut into small pieces
- 2 tablespoons (20 g) flaxseeds
- 1 ½ cups (375 g) ice cubes

METHOD

- Place the coconut water, coconut milk, banana, flaxseeds, and ice cubes in a blender. Process until smooth.
- Pour in individual glasses. Garnish with banana slices.
- Serve immediately and enjoy.

NUTRITIONAL INFORMATION

Energy	Fat	Carbohydrates	Protein	Sodium
215 calories	8.9 g	34.1 g	3.5 g	133 mg

KIWI BANANA AND PINEAPPLE SHAKE

Preparation Time	Total Time	Yield
5 minutes	5 minutes	4 servings

INGREDIENTS

- 3 medium kiwi fruit (about 80 g each), cut into small pieces
- 2 medium banana (about 120 g each), cut into small pieces
- 1 cup (240 ml) pineapple juice
- 2 cups (500 g) crushed ice

METHOD

- Place the kiwi fruit, banana, pineapple juice, and crushed ice in a blender. Process until smooth.
- Pour in serving glasses. Garnish with kiwi slices.
- Serve immediately and enjoy.

NUTRITIONAL INFORMATION

Energy	Fat	Carbohydrates	Protein	Sodium
120 calories	0.6 g	29.9 g	1.5 g	4 mg

STRAWBERRY CHERRY AND ALMOND SMOOTHIE

Preparation Time	Total Time	Yield
5 minutes	5 minutes	4 servings

INGREDIENTS

- 2 cups (440 g) strawberries, hulled
- 2 cup (300 g) fresh red cherries, pitted
- 1 cup (240 ml) almond milk
- 1/4 cup (80 ml) honey
- 1 ½ cups (375 g) ice cubes
- Cherries, for garnish
- Mint sprigs, for garnish

METHOD

- Place the strawberries, cherries, almond milk, honey, and ice cubes in a blender. Process until smooth.
- Pour in serving glasses. Garnish with cherries and mint sprigs.
- Serve immediately and enjoy.

NUTRITIONAL INFORMATION

Energy	Fat	Carbohydrates	Protein	Sodium
133 calories	1.1 g	32.7 g	1.6 g	39 mg

MANGO BANANA AND GINGER LASSI

Preparation Time	Total Time	Yield
5 minutes	5 minutes	4 servings

INGREDIENTS

- 2 cups (330 g) mango, diced
- 1 medium (120 g) banana, sliced
- 1 cup (240 ml) whole milk
- 6 ounces (180 g) Greek yogurt
- 2 teaspoons (6 g) fresh ginger, grated
- 1 ½ cups (375 g) ice cubes
- Diced mango, for garnish
- Fresh mint sprigs

METHOD

- Place the mango, banana, milk, yogurt, ginger, and ice cubes in a blender. Process until smooth.
- Pour in serving glasses. Garnish with diced mango and mint sprigs.
- Serve immediately and enjoy.

NUTRITIONAL INFORMATION

Energy	Fat	Carbohydrates	Protein	Sodium
172 calories	3.8 g	27.5 g	9.4 g	73 mg

PINEAPPLE KIWI AND COCONUT SHAKE

Preparation Time	Total Time	Yield
5 minutes	5 minutes	4 servings

INGREDIENTS

- 2 cups (330 g) pineapple, cubed
- 2 medium kiwi fruit (about 80 g each), sliced
- 2 cups (480 ml) coconut water
- 1 ½ cups (375 g) ice cubes
- Honey, to taste
- Fresh mint sprigs, for garnish

METHOD

- Place the pineapple, kiwi fruit, coconut water, and ice cubes in a blender. Drizzle some honey to taste. Process until smooth.
- Pour in serving glasses. Garnish with mint sprigs.
- Serve immediately and enjoy.

NUTRITIONAL INFORMATION

Energy	Fat	Carbohydrates	Protein	Sodium
135 calories	0.5 g	33.8 g	1.8 g	129 mg

MANGO BANANA AND CINNAMON BLAST

Preparation Time	Total Time	Yield
5 minutes	5 minutes	4 servings

INGREDIENTS

- 2 cups (330 g) mango, cut into cubes
- 2 medium banana (about 120 g each), sliced
- 2 cups (480 ml) whole milk
- 1 teaspoon (2 g) cinnamon, ground
- 1 ½ cups (375 g) ice cubes

METHOD

- Combine mango, banana, milk, cinnamon, and ice cubes in a blender. Process until smooth. Pour in serving glasses. Garnish with a slice of mango and sprinkle with some cinnamon on top, if desired.
- Serve immediately and enjoy.

NUTRITIONAL INFORMATION

Energy	Fat	Carbohydrates	Protein	Sodium
164 calories	3.0 g	32.3 g	5.3 g	59 mg

DRAGON FRUIT MANGO AND BANANA SMOOTHIE

Preparation Time	Total Time	Yield
5 minutes	5 minutes	4 servings

INGREDIENTS

- 2 medium dragon fruit (about 200 g each), diced
- 1 cup (165 g) mango, diced
- 1 medium (120 g) banana, sliced
- 2 cups (480 ml) almond milk
- 1 ½ cups (375 g) ice cubes
- Mint sprigs, for garnish

METHOD

- Place the dragon fruit, mango, banana, almond milk, and ice cubes in a blender. Process until smooth.
- Pour in serving glasses. Garnish with mint sprigs.
- Serve immediately and enjoy.

NUTRITIONAL INFORMATION

Energy	Fat	Carbohydrates	Protein	Sodium
124 calories	1.5 g	26.4 g	2.2 g	76 mg

MANGO PINEAPPLE AND BANANA SMOOTHIE

Preparation Time	Total Time	Yield
5 minutes	5 minutes	4 servings

INGREDIENTS

- 2 cups (330 g) mango, cubed
- 1 ½ cups (250 g) pineapple, cubed
- 1 medium (120 g) banana, sliced
- 2 cups (480 ml) coconut water
- 1 ½ cups (375 g) ice cubes

METHOD

- Place the mango, pineapple, banana, coconut water, and ice cubes in a blender. Process until smooth.
- Pour in serving glasses. Garnish with mango or pineapple slices if desired.
- Serve immediately and enjoy.

NUTRITIONAL INFORMATION

Energy	Fat	Carbohydrates	Protein	Sodium
129 calories	0.7 g	31.7 g	2.2 g	128 mg

KIWI PINEAPPLE AND YOGURT SMOOTHIE

Preparation Time	Total Time	Yield
5 minutes	5 minutes	4 servings

INGREDIENTS

- 4 medium kiwi fruit (about 80 g each), sliced
- 1 cup (165 g) pineapple, cubed
- 6 ounces (180 g) Greek yogurt
- 1 ½ cups (360 ml) almond milk
- 1 ½ cups (375 g) ice cubes
- Kiwi slices, for garnish

METHOD

- Place the kiwi fruit, pineapple, yogurt, almond milk, and ice cubes in a blender. Process until smooth.
- Pour in serving glasses. Garnish with kiwi slices.
- Serve immediately and enjoy.

NUTRITIONAL INFORMATION

Energy	Fat	Carbohydrates	Protein	Sodium
121 calories	2.3 g	21.4 g	5.9 g	73 mg

MANGO STRAWBERRY AND YOGURT SMOOTHIE

Preparation Time	Total Time	Yield
5 minutes	5 minutes	4 servings

INGREDIENTS

- 2 cups (330 g) mango, cubed
- 1 cup (200 g) strawberries, hulled
- 6 ounces (180 g) Greek yogurt, vanilla flavor
- 1 cup (240 ml) whole milk
- 1 ½ cups (375 g) ice cubes
- Honey, to taste
- Strawberries and mango slices, for garnish

METHOD

- Place the mango, strawberries, yogurt, milk, and ice cubes in a blender. Drizzle some honey to taste. Process until smooth.
- Pour in serving glasses. Garnish with strawberries or mango slices if desired.
- Serve immediately and enjoy.

NUTRITIONAL INFORMATION

Energy	Fat	Carbohydrates	Protein	Sodium
156 calories	2.5 g	28.5 g	7.2 g	44 mg

MELON BANANA AND ALMOND SMOOTHIE

Preparation Time	Total Time	Yield
5 minutes	5 minutes	4 servings

INGREDIENTS

- 3 cups (340 g) rock melon or cantaloupe, cubed
- 2 medium banana (about 120 g each), sliced
- 2 cups (480 ml) almond milk
- 1 ½ cups (375 g) ice cubes
- Honey, to taste
- Fresh mint sprigs, for garnish

METHOD

- Combine the rock melon, banana, almond milk, and ice cubes ice in a blender. Drizzle some honey to taste. Process until smooth.
- Pour in serving glasses. Garnish with mint sprigs.
- Serve immediately and enjoy.

NUTRITIONAL INFORMATION

Energy	Fat	Carbohydrates	Protein	Sodium
139 calories	1.7 g	32.2g	2.2 g	95 mg

BERRY PINEAPPLE AND YOGURT SMOOTHIE

Preparation Time	Total Time	Yield
5 minutes	5 minutes	4 servings

INGREDIENTS

- 1 cup (170 g) frozen blueberries
- 1 cup (140 g) frozen raspberries
- 1 cup (165 g) pineapple, cubed
- 6 ounces (180 g) Greek yogurt
- 2 cups (480 ml) almond milk
- 2 tablespoons (40 ml) maple syrup
- Mixed berries, for garnish

METHOD

- Place the frozen berries, pineapple, yogurt, almond milk, and maple syrup in a blender. Process until smooth.
- Pour in serving glasses. Garnish with some berries.
- Serve immediately and enjoy.

NUTRITIONAL INFORMATION

Energy	Fat	Carbohydrates	Protein	Sodium
130 calories	2.5 g	23.3 g	5.7 g	91 mg

ORANGE BANANA AND YOGURT SHAKE

Preparation Time	Total Time	Yield
5 minutes	5 minutes	4 servings

INGREDIENTS

- 4 medium banana (about 120 g each), sliced
- 3/4 cup (180 ml) fresh orange juice
- 6 ounces (180 g) Greek yogurt
- 1 cup (240 ml) almond milk
- 1 ½ cups (375 g) ice cubes
- Orange slices, to serve

METHOD

- Place the banana, orange, yogurt, almond milk, and ice cubes in a blender. Process until smooth.
- Pour in serving glasses. Garnish with orange slices.
- Serve immediately and enjoy.

NUTRITIONAL INFORMATION

Energy	Fat	Carbohydrates	Protein	Sodium
159 calories	1.9 g	32.1 g	6.0 g	53 mg

PEACH STRAWBERRY AND YOGURT SMOOTHIE

Preparation Time	Total Time	Yield
5 minutes	5 minutes	4 servings

INGREDIENTS

- 3 cups (450 g) peaches, diced
- 1 cup (200 g) fresh strawberries, hulled
- 1 cup (240 ml) whole milk
- 6 ounces (180 g) Greek yogurt
- 1 ½ cups (375 g) ice cubes
- Honey, to taste
- Strawberries, for garnish

METHOD

- Place the peaches, strawberries, milk, yogurt, and ice cubes in a blender. Drizzle some honey to taste. Process until smooth.
- Pour in serving glasses. Garnish with strawberries.
- Serve immediately and enjoy.

NUTRITIONAL INFORMATION

Energy	Fat	Carbohydrates	Protein	Sodium
150 calories	2.5 g	26.6 g	7.6 g	43 mg

PLUM KIWI AND PINEAPPLE SMOOTHIE

Preparation Time	Total Time	Yield
5 minutes	5 minutes	4 servings

INGREDIENTS

- 4 medium plum (about 70 g each), cut into small pieces
- 2 medium kiwi fruit (about 80 g each), cut into small pieces
- 1 cup (240 ml) pineapple juice
- 6 ounces (180 g) Greek yogurt
- 1 ½ cups (375 g) ice cubes

METHOD

- Place the plum, kiwi, pineapple juice, yogurt, and ice cubes in a blender. Process until smooth.
- Pour in serving glasses.
- Serve immediately and enjoy.

NUTRITIONAL INFORMATION

Energy	Fat	Carbohydrates	Protein	Sodium
118 calories	1.3 g	23.3 g	5.5 g	16 mg

STRAWBERRY KIWI AND BANANA SHAKE

Preparation Time	Total Time	Yield
5 minutes	5 minutes	4 servings

INGREDIENTS

- 2 cups (440 g) frozen strawberries, hulled
- 2 medium kiwi fruit (about 80 g each), cut into small pieces
- 1 medium (120 g) banana, sliced
- 2 cups (480 ml) whole milk
- Fresh mint sprigs, for garnish
- Strawberries, for garnish

METHOD

- Place the strawberries, kiwi, banana, and milk in a blender. Process until smooth.
- Pour in serving glasses. Garnish with strawberries and mint sprigs.
- Serve immediately and enjoy.

NUTRITIONAL INFORMATION

Energy	Fat	Carbohydrates	Protein	Sodium
133 calories	3.0 g	23.8 g	5.2 g	60 mg

TROPICAL BANANA PINEAPPLE SMOOTHIE

Preparation Time	Total Time	Yield
5 minutes	5 minutes	4 servings

INGREDIENTS

- 3 medium banana (about 120 g each), sliced
- 2 cup (330 g) pineapple, cubed
- 1 cup (240 ml) coconut water
- 1/2 cup (120 ml) coconut milk
- 1 ½ cups (375 g) ice cubes
- Mint sprigs, for garnish
- Pineapple chunks, for garnish

METHOD

- Place the banana, pineapple, coconut water, coconut milk, and ice cubes in a blender. Process until smooth.
- Pour in chilled tall glasses. Garnish with pineapple chunks and mint sprigs.
- Serve immediately and enjoy.

NUTRITIONAL INFORMATION

Energy	Fat	Carbohydrates	Protein	Sodium
200 calories	7.7 g	34.9 g	2.5 g	69 mg

PEACH STRAWBERRY AND BANANA SMOOTHIE

Preparation Time	Total Time	Yield
5 minutes	5 minutes	4 servings

INGREDIENTS

- 2 cups (300 g) peaches, cubed
- 1 cup (220 g) frozen strawberries, hulled
- 1 medium (120 g) banana, sliced
- 2 cups (480 ml) whole milk
- Fresh mint sprigs, for garnish
- Peach slices, for garnish

METHOD

- Place the peach, strawberries, banana, and milk in a blender. Process until smooth.
- Pour in serving glasses. Garnish with peach slices and mint sprigs.
- Serve immediately and enjoy.

NUTRITIONAL INFORMATION

Energy	Fat	Carbohydrates	Protein	Sodium
141 calories	4.3 g	22.5 g	5.0 g	49 mg

VANILLA ORANGE AND PINEAPPLE SMOOTHIE

Preparation Time	Total Time	Yield
5 minutes	5 minutes	4 servings

INGREDIENTS

- 1 cup (245 g) vanilla yogurt
- 1 cup (240 ml) almond milk
- 1 cup (200 g) orange segments
- 1 cup (165 g) pineapple, cubed
- 1 ½ cups (375 g) ice cubes
- Honey, to taste
- Orange slices, for garnish

METHOD

- Place the yogurt, almond milk, orange segments, pineapple, and ice cubes in a blender. Drizzle some honey to taste. Process until smooth.
- Pour in individual glasses. Garnish with orange slices.
- Serve immediately and enjoy.

NUTRITIONAL INFORMATION

Energy	Fat	Carbohydrates	Protein	Sodium
125 calories	1.5 g	23.9 g	4.4 g	81 mg

BLACKBERRY BANANA AND YOGURT SHAKE

Preparation Time	Total Time	Yield
5 minutes	5 minutes	4 servings

INGREDIENTS

- 2 cups (340 g) frozen blackberries
- 2 medium banana (about 120 g each), sliced
- 1 cup (245 g) Greek yogurt, vanilla flavor
- 1 ½ cups (360 ml) whole milk
- 2 tablespoons (40 ml) maple syrup
- Blackberries, for garnish

METHOD

- Place the blackberries, banana, yogurt, milk, and maple syrup in a blender. Process until smooth.
- Pour in chilled serving glasses. Garnish with blackberries.
- Serve immediately and enjoy.

NUTRITIONAL INFORMATION

Energy	Fat	Carbohydrates	Protein	Sodium
193 calories	3.4 g	33.6 g	9.6 g	62 mg

RECIPE INDEX

Minty Strawberry Lemon Lime Soda 22

O

Orange and Apple Cooler with Mint 25
Orange Banana and Yogurt Shake 79

P

Papaya and Lime Cooler with Honey 36
Papaya Pineapple and Lime Slushy 53
Peach Strawberry and Banana Smoothie 84
Peach Strawberry and Yogurt Smoothie 80
Pineapple Coconut and Lemon Slushy 56
Pineapple Kiwi and Coconut Shake 71
Pineapple Lemon Cooler with Mint 27
Pineapple Orange and Coconut Slushy 58
Pink Rose and Lemon Infused Water 20
Pink Rose Lemonade 12
Plum Kiwi and Pineapple Smoothie 81

R

Raspberry and Lemon Infused Water 17
Red Currant Cherry and Strawberry Slushy 52

S

Sparkling Peach and Lime Mocktail 8
Sparkling Strawberry Limeade 14
Sparkling Watermelon and Strawberry Cooler 26
Strawberry and Mint Infused Water 19
Strawberry and Pomegranate Slushy 54
Strawberry Banana and Coconut Shake 65
Strawberry Cherry and Almond Smoothie 69
Strawberry Iced Tea 47
Strawberry Kiwi and Banana Shake 82
Strawberry Rose and Lime Mocktail 9

T

Tropical Banana Pineapple Smoothie 83
Tropical Citrus Cooler 28

V

Vanilla Orange and Pineapple Smoothie 85

W

Watermelon Cucumber Slushy 49
Watermelon Lime Cooler with Agave 30
Watermelon Orange and Pineapple Slushy 57

We want to thank you for purchasing this book.
Our writers and creative team took pride in
creating this book, and we have tried to make it as
enjoyable as possible.

We would love to hear from you. Kindly leave
us a review if you enjoyed this book so we can
do more. Your reviews on our books are highly
appreciated. Also, if you have any comments
or suggestions, you may reach us at info@
contentarcade.com

Regards,
Content Arcade Publishing Team

Made in the USA
Monee, IL
11 May 2023